# Under Fire: The War in Ukraine

*Chronicle of Occupation, Resistance, and Resilience*

David Greed

## Description

Under Fire: The War in Ukraine is a gripping and thought-provoking chronicle of one of the most devastating conflicts of our time. Through a combination of eyewitness accounts, in-depth analysis, and historical context, this book offers a comprehensive and nuanced understanding of the war in Ukraine.

From the Russian annexation of Crimea to the occupation of Donbas and the formation of Ukrainian volunteer battalions, this book delves into the causes and early stages of the conflict. It also examines the humanitarian crisis and displacement that have resulted from the conflict, as well as the role of international support and civil society resistance against occupation.

But this book is not just a recounting of events - it is also a powerful reflection on the trauma and coping mechanisms of those affected by the conflict. It explores the social and economic impacts of the war, as well as the lessons learned and prospects for resolution and peace.

Under Fire is not just a book for those interested in the conflict in Ukraine - it is a book for anyone who wants to understand the complex and interconnected issues that shape our world today. It is a must-read for anyone who cares about the human toll of war and the prospects for building a more just and peaceful world.

BACKGROUND INFORMATION ON THE CONFLICT IN UKRAINE ........................... ERRORE. IL SEGNALIBRO NON È DEFINITO.

PURPOSE OF THE BOOK ............................................................. 8

CAUSES AND EARLY STAGES OF THE CONFLICT .......................... 12

RUSSIAN ANNEXATION OF CRIMEA ............................................ 18

OCCUPATION OF DONBAS ........................................................ 21

HUMANITARIAN CRISIS AND DISPLACEMENT ............................ 26

FORMATION OF UKRAINIAN VOLUNTEER BATTALIONS ............. 32

ROLE OF INTERNATIONAL SUPPORT ......................................... 41

CIVIL SOCIETY RESISTANCE AGAINST OCCUPATION ................... 44

SOCIAL AND ECONOMIC IMPACTS OF THE CONFLICT ................ 48

ADAPTATION TO THE NEW REALITY .......................................... 50

COMMUNITY BUILDING AND SOLIDARITY ................................. 54

LESSONS LEARNED AND RECOMMENDATIONS .......................... 71

REFLECTIONS ON THE WAR AND ITS CONSEQUENCES ............... 76

FINAL THOUGHTS AND CALL TO ACTION .................................. 80

# Background information on the conflict in Ukraine

The conflict in Ukraine is a complex and multi-faceted issue that has its roots in the country's history, culture, and geopolitical position. The conflict began in 2014, following the Ukrainian Revolution of 2014, which resulted in the ousting of President Viktor Yanukovych. The revolution was sparked by Yanukovych's decision to back out of a deal with the European Union in favor of closer ties with Russia, which was seen as a betrayal of Ukraine's pro-European aspirations.

The revolution was met with a violent response from the Yanukovych government, resulting in the deaths of over 100 protestors. This led to a popular uprising, which forced Yanukovych to flee the country, and the establishment of a new government in Kyiv.

The events of 2014 set the stage for the conflict that followed, as Russia saw the Ukrainian Revolution as a threat to its interests in the region. Russia's annexation of Crimea in March 2014 was the first step in what would become a larger conflict between Ukraine and Russia.

The annexation of Crimea was met with international condemnation, and the United States and European Union imposed economic sanctions on Russia in response. However, Russia continued to support separatist movements in eastern Ukraine, which led to the outbreak of fighting in the Donbas region.

The conflict in eastern Ukraine has been characterized by a mix of conventional and unconventional warfare, with Ukrainian government forces fighting against separatist militias backed by Russian forces. The conflict has resulted in the deaths of over 13,000 people, including civilians, and has displaced over 1.6 million people.

The situation in Ukraine is further complicated by the presence of various political, social, and cultural divisions within the country. Ukraine is a diverse country, with a mix of Ukrainian and Russian speakers, and a history of regionalism and ethnic tensions. These divisions have been exploited by both the Ukrainian and Russian governments in their efforts to gain support for their respective positions.

The conflict in Ukraine has also had a significant impact on the country's economy and social fabric. The war has resulted in the destruction of infrastructure and the disruption of trade, leading to a sharp decline in economic activity. The humanitarian crisis in the conflict zone has also led to widespread suffering and displacement, with many people struggling to access basic necessities such as food, water, and healthcare.

The conflict in Ukraine has had significant implications for regional and global security. The annexation of Crimea has challenged the post-Cold War order in Europe and raised questions about the durability of international norms and institutions. The conflict in eastern Ukraine has also raised concerns about the risk of a wider war between Russia and the West.

Efforts to resolve the conflict in Ukraine have been ongoing since 2014, but have thus far been unsuccessful. Diplomatic efforts have been hampered by a lack of trust between the parties, as well as the involvement of outside actors such as Russia and the United States.

In conclusion, the conflict in Ukraine is a complex and multi-faceted issue that has its roots in the country's history, culture, and geopolitical position. The conflict has resulted in significant human suffering, economic disruption, and security implications, and continues to be a major challenge for the international community.

# Purpose of the book

"Under Fire: The War in Ukraine: A Chronicle of Occupation, Resistance, and Resilience" is a book that aims to provide a comprehensive and nuanced understanding of the conflict in Ukraine. The purpose of this book is to go beyond the headlines and soundbites that dominate media coverage of the conflict, and to provide readers with a deeper understanding of the political, social, and cultural dynamics that underlie the conflict.

One of the key purposes of this book is to provide a platform for the voices of those who have been directly affected by the conflict in Ukraine. This includes Ukrainian civilians who have been displaced by the fighting, as well as members of the Ukrainian military and volunteer battalions who have fought on the frontlines. By giving voice to these individuals, the book aims to humanize the conflict and to provide readers with a sense of the lived experience of those who have been impacted by the conflict.

Another key purpose of this book is to explore the various factors that have contributed to the conflict in Ukraine. This includes an examination of the historical, cultural, and geopolitical factors that have shaped the conflict, as well as an analysis of the actions of the various actors involved, including the Ukrainian government, the separatist militias, and external actors such as Russia and the United States. By providing a nuanced understanding of the conflict, the book aims to challenge simplistic narratives that reduce the conflict to a binary struggle between Ukraine and Russia.

The book also aims to provide a critical analysis of the international response to the conflict in Ukraine. This includes an examination of the diplomatic efforts to resolve the conflict, as well as an analysis of the role of international institutions such as the United Nations and the European Union. The book seeks to provide readers with a critical perspective on the limitations of international interventions in conflict situations, and to explore alternative approaches to conflict resolution.

One of the key themes of the book is the concept of resilience. The conflict in Ukraine has had a profound impact on Ukrainian society, but it has also given rise to a remarkable spirit of resilience among those affected by the conflict. The book aims to explore this theme by highlighting the stories of individuals and communities who have shown remarkable strength and determination in the face of adversity.

Finally, the book aims to contribute to broader discussions about the nature of conflict and the prospects for peace. By examining the conflict in Ukraine in detail, the book aims to provide readers with a deeper understanding of the causes and consequences of conflict, as well as the challenges and opportunities for resolving conflict. The book also aims to highlight the importance of dialogue, understanding, and empathy in addressing the root causes of conflict and building a more peaceful and just world.

In conclusion, the purpose of "Under Fire: The War in Ukraine: A Chronicle of Occupation, Resistance, and Resilience" is to provide readers with a comprehensive and nuanced understanding of the conflict in Ukraine, and to contribute to broader discussions about the nature of conflict and the prospects for peace. The book aims to provide a platform for the voices of those affected by the conflict, to explore the various factors that have contributed to the conflict, and to highlight the importance of resilience, dialogue, and empathy in addressing the root causes of conflict.

# Causes and early stages of the conflict

The conflict in Ukraine has its roots in a complex set of historical, cultural, and geopolitical factors. To understand the conflict, it is necessary to look back at the events that preceded it and to consider the factors that contributed to its outbreak.

Historical context

The history of Ukraine is complex and multifaceted, and its people have faced many challenges throughout their history. Ukraine has been subject to numerous invasions and occupations, including by the Mongols, Poles, Ottoman Turks, and Russians. Despite this history of foreign domination, Ukraine has maintained a distinct culture and identity, and its people have shown remarkable resilience in the face of adversity.

One of the key events in Ukraine's modern history was the collapse of the Soviet Union in 1991. Following the collapse of the Soviet Union, Ukraine declared its independence, and a new era of Ukrainian history began. However, the transition to independence was not without its challenges, and

Ukraine struggled to establish a stable political and economic system.

Geopolitical context

Ukraine's geopolitical position has also played a role in the conflict. Ukraine is situated at the crossroads of Europe and Asia, and its strategic location has made it a target for various external powers throughout history. In recent years, Ukraine has become a battleground in the geopolitical struggle between the West and Russia.

The conflict in Ukraine began in 2014, following a series of events that shook the country and led to the overthrow of the Ukrainian government. The events that triggered the conflict can be traced back to the decision of the Ukrainian government to suspend negotiations on a trade agreement with the European Union (EU) in November 2013. This decision was met with widespread protests in Ukraine, as many Ukrainians saw closer ties with the EU as a way to move the country closer to Western values and standards.

Maidan protests

The protests, which became known as the Euromaidan protests, lasted for several months and eventually led to the overthrow of Ukrainian President Viktor Yanukovych in February 2014. Yanukovych, who had close ties to Russia, was replaced by a pro-Western government led by Arseniy Yatsenyuk. The events of the Euromaidan protests and the subsequent overthrow of Yanukovych were widely seen as a victory for democracy and Western values.

However, the events also had significant implications for Ukraine's relationship with Russia. Russia saw the events in Ukraine as a direct challenge to its interests in the region, and it responded by annexing Crimea, a Ukrainian territory with a significant Russian-speaking population, in March 2014. This move was widely condemned by the international community, and it set the stage for the conflict that was to follow.

Donbas insurgency

In the aftermath of the annexation of Crimea, pro-Russian separatists in the Donbas region of eastern Ukraine began to seize control of government buildings and declare the creation of the Donetsk People's Republic and the Luhansk People's Republic. The Ukrainian government responded by launching a military operation to retake control of the territory, and the conflict quickly escalated into a full-scale war.

The conflict in Ukraine has been characterized by its complexity and its shifting alliances. The Ukrainian government has been supported by Western countries such as the United States and the European Union, while the separatist militias have been supported by Russia. The conflict has also been marked by allegations of human rights abuses on both sides, as well as reports of widespread corruption and criminal activity.

Conclusion

In conclusion, the conflict in Ukraine has its roots in a complex set of historical, cultural, and geopolitical factors. The decision by the Ukrainian government to suspend negotiations on a trade agreement with the European Union was the trigger for the conflict, but the underlying causes go much deeper. The conflict has been

# Russian annexation of Crimea

The Russian annexation of Crimea in 2014 was a major turning point in the conflict in Ukraine. The annexation, which was widely condemned by the international community, sparked a new phase in the conflict and heightened tensions between Russia and Western countries.

Background

Crimea is a peninsula located in the Black Sea, and it has a long and complex history. Crimea was part of Russia until 1954 when it was transferred to the Ukrainian Soviet Socialist Republic. Following the collapse of the Soviet Union, Crimea became part of independent Ukraine.

Despite being part of Ukraine, Crimea has a significant Russian-speaking population, and many Crimeans feel a strong connection to Russia. The issue of Crimea's status has been a source of tension between Ukraine and Russia for many years.

### Events leading up to annexation

The events that led to the annexation of Crimea can be traced back to the Euromaidan protests in Ukraine in 2013-2014. As mentioned earlier, the protests resulted in the overthrow of Ukrainian President Viktor Yanukovych, who had close ties to Russia.

The events of the Euromaidan protests were seen as a direct challenge to Russia's interests in the region, and Russia responded by annexing Crimea in March 2014. Russian President Vladimir Putin justified the annexation by citing the need to protect Russian-speaking minorities in Crimea and by accusing the Ukrainian government of being illegitimate.

### International reaction

The annexation of Crimea was widely condemned by the international community, and the United Nations General Assembly passed a resolution affirming Ukraine's territorial integrity and condemning the annexation. The United States and the European Union imposed economic sanctions on Russia in response to the annexation, and tensions between Russia and the West increased.

Impact on the conflict

The annexation of Crimea had a significant impact on the conflict in Ukraine. It led to the outbreak of fighting in eastern Ukraine, as pro-Russian separatists in the Donbas region of Ukraine began to seize control of government buildings and declare the creation of the Donetsk People's Republic and the Luhansk People's Republic.

The annexation of Crimea also led to a shift in the balance of power in the region, with Russia gaining a strategic foothold in the Black Sea. The annexation was a significant blow to Ukraine's territorial integrity and sovereignty, and it undermined the international legal order.

Conclusion

The Russian annexation of Crimea was a major turning point in the conflict in Ukraine, and it had significant implications for the region and for international relations. The annexation was widely condemned by the international community, and it led to a new phase in the conflict in eastern Ukraine. The annexation also had a significant impact on the balance of power in the region, and it undermined the international legal order. The annexation of Crimea remains a contentious issue, and its legacy will continue to shape the political landscape of the region for years to come.

# Occupation of Donbas

The occupation of Donbas, a region in eastern Ukraine, has been a key aspect of the conflict in Ukraine. The occupation, which began in 2014, has resulted in a significant loss of life and displacement, and has had profound political and economic consequences for Ukraine.

Background

The Donbas region is comprised of two provinces - Donetsk and Luhansk - and it has a long history of industrial development. Donetsk was a major center for coal mining and heavy industry during the Soviet period, and Luhansk was known for its machine-building and metallurgical industries. The region has a significant Russian-speaking population and has long been a focal point of tensions between Ukraine and Russia.

Occupation

In April 2014, pro-Russian separatists in the Donbas region declared the creation of the Donetsk People's Republic and the Luhansk People's Republic, and began to seize control of government buildings and infrastructure. The Ukrainian government responded by launching a military operation to retake control of the region, which resulted in a protracted conflict.

The conflict has been characterized by intermittent fighting and ceasefire agreements, and has resulted in a significant loss of life and displacement. The United Nations estimates that over 13,000 people have been killed and over 1.5 million people have been displaced as a result of the conflict.

Impact

The occupation of Donbas has had a profound impact on Ukraine. The conflict has devastated the region's economy, with many factories and businesses being destroyed or forced to close. The conflict has also had political consequences, with the occupation leading to a shift in the political landscape of Ukraine.

The occupation has also had significant implications for international relations. The conflict has been widely viewed as a proxy war between

Russia and the West, with Russia being accused of providing military and financial support to the separatists in the Donbas region. The conflict has led to a deterioration in relations between Russia and the West, with economic sanctions being imposed on Russia in response to its actions.

Attempts at resolution

Efforts to resolve the conflict have been ongoing, with various ceasefire agreements being reached and diplomatic initiatives being pursued. The Minsk agreements, which were signed in 2015, called for a ceasefire, the withdrawal of heavy weapons, and the creation of a special status for the Donbas region. However, the implementation of the agreements has been slow and incomplete, and fighting has continued.

Conclusion

The occupation of Donbas has been a key aspect of the conflict in Ukraine, and has had profound political, economic, and humanitarian consequences. The conflict has resulted in a significant loss of life and displacement, and has led to a deterioration in international relations. The conflict remains unresolved, and its legacy will continue to shape the political landscape of the region for years to come. The international community must continue to support efforts to find a peaceful resolution to the conflict and to address the humanitarian needs of those affected by the conflict.

# Humanitarian crisis and displacement

The conflict in Ukraine has resulted in a significant humanitarian crisis, with millions of people affected by displacement, loss of livelihoods, and a breakdown in basic services such as healthcare and education. The conflict has had a profound impact on the lives of individuals and communities, and has created a significant challenge for the international community in providing humanitarian assistance and addressing the root causes of the crisis.

Background

Since the outbreak of the conflict in 2014, the humanitarian situation in Ukraine has deteriorated significantly. The conflict has resulted in a significant loss of life, with over 13,000 people killed and tens of thousands injured. The conflict has also displaced over 1.5 million people within Ukraine, and has forced an estimated 1.4 million people to flee to neighboring countries.

Displacement

The displacement of people has been a major consequence of the conflict in Ukraine. Many people have been forced to flee their homes due to the fighting, with some seeking refuge in other parts of Ukraine and others crossing the border into neighboring countries such as Russia, Belarus, and Poland. The displacement of people has had a profound impact on the lives of those affected, with many losing their homes, possessions, and livelihoods.

The displacement of people has also created a significant challenge for humanitarian organizations and governments, who have struggled to provide assistance and support to those affected. The provision of basic services such as shelter, food, and healthcare has been a major challenge, with many people living in temporary accommodation and struggling to access healthcare and other services.

Humanitarian assistance

Humanitarian assistance has been a critical response to the crisis in Ukraine, with international organizations and governments providing support to those affected by the conflict. The provision of assistance has included the distribution of food, shelter, and other basic necessities, as well as the provision of healthcare and education services.

However, the provision of humanitarian assistance has been hampered by a range of challenges, including access constraints, bureaucratic hurdles, and funding gaps. Many areas affected by the conflict are difficult to access due to fighting and insecurity, and bureaucratic procedures can be cumbersome and slow. In addition, funding for humanitarian assistance has been insufficient, with many organizations struggling to meet the needs of those affected.

## Human rights violations

The conflict in Ukraine has also resulted in a range of human rights violations, including arbitrary detention, torture, and enforced disappearances. Both sides of the conflict have been accused of human rights abuses, including the separatists in the Donbas region and Ukrainian government forces.

The humanitarian crisis in Ukraine has been exacerbated by these human rights abuses, which have contributed to a breakdown in the rule of law and a lack of accountability for those responsible for abuses. The provision of humanitarian assistance has also been hampered by these abuses, with humanitarian workers being targeted and harassed.

## Conclusion

The humanitarian crisis in Ukraine is a major consequence of the conflict, and has had a profound impact on the lives of individuals and communities. The displacement of people has been a major challenge, with many people losing their homes and struggling to access basic services. The provision of humanitarian assistance has been critical in addressing the needs of those affected, but has been hampered by a range of challenges.

The international community must continue to support efforts to address the humanitarian crisis in Ukraine, including the provision of humanitarian assistance, support for those affected by displacement, and efforts to address the root causes of the crisis. This includes efforts to address human rights abuses and promote accountability for those responsible, as well as support for the political and economic reform needed to address the underlying causes of the conflict. Ultimately, the humanitarian crisis in Ukraine can only be addressed through a sustained and comprehensive response by the international community.

# Formation of Ukrainian volunteer battalions

The conflict in Ukraine has been marked by the formation of a large number of volunteer battalions, which have played a significant role in the fighting against separatist forces in the Donbas region. These battalions have been formed by a range of groups, including political parties, civil society organizations, and private citizens, and have been motivated by a range of factors, including patriotism, a desire to protect their communities, and a sense of frustration with the government's response to the conflict.

Background

The formation of volunteer battalions in Ukraine can be traced back to the early stages of the conflict, when the Ukrainian government was struggling to respond to the seizure of government buildings in the Crimean Peninsula by Russian-backed separatist forces. In the absence of a strong government response, a range of groups began to mobilize in support of the government and in opposition to the separatists.

These early efforts to mobilize volunteers were largely informal and disorganized, with groups of individuals gathering together to form ad hoc militias. However, as the conflict escalated and spread to the Donbas region, these groups began to coalesce into more formal volunteer battalions, with the support of the government and military authorities.

Formation of volunteer battalions

The formation of volunteer battalions in Ukraine has been motivated by a range of factors. For some, the decision to join a volunteer battalion was motivated by a sense of patriotic duty, a desire to defend their country and protect their communities from separatist forces. Others were motivated by a sense of frustration with the government's response to the conflict, feeling that the government was not doing enough to protect its citizens.

Many of these battalions were formed by political parties, civil society organizations, and private citizens, with the support of the Ukrainian military and government. These groups provided training, equipment, and funding for the battalions, as well as support for their families.

The battalions themselves were organized into units, with each unit having a specific area of responsibility or mission. The units were made up of volunteers from a range of backgrounds, including military veterans, students, and professionals, and were often organized along regional or ethnic lines.

Role in the conflict

The volunteer battalions in Ukraine have played a significant role in the fighting against separatist forces in the Donbas region. These battalions have been involved in a range of military operations, including defending key cities and strategic locations, conducting reconnaissance and intelligence gathering, and carrying out offensive operations against separatist forces.

The battalions have been praised for their bravery and commitment, and have been credited with playing a key role in pushing back separatist forces and retaking territory. However, they have also been criticized for their lack of discipline and accountability, with reports of human rights abuses and extrajudicial killings.

Impact on society

The formation of volunteer battalions in Ukraine has had a significant impact on Ukrainian society, both positive and negative. On the one hand, the battalions have provided a sense of community and purpose for their members, and have been seen as a symbol of national unity and pride.

On the other hand, the formation of these battalions has also highlighted the weaknesses of the Ukrainian state, including its inability to provide for the security of its citizens and its reliance on informal and ad hoc groups to fill the gap. The battalions have also been criticized for their lack of accountability and transparency, with concerns about human rights abuses and corruption.

## Conclusion

The formation of volunteer battalions in Ukraine has been a significant aspect of the conflict, reflecting the deep divisions within Ukrainian society and the weaknesses of the Ukrainian state. While these battalions have played a key role in the fighting against separatist forces, they have also raised concerns about human rights abuses and extrajudicial killings

Military operations and tactics

The conflict in Ukraine has been marked by a range of military operations and tactics, as both Ukrainian government forces and separatist forces have sought to gain control over territory and assert their dominance. This section will provide an overview of some of the key military operations and tactics employed in the conflict.

Urban warfare: One of the defining features of the conflict in Ukraine has been the prevalence of urban warfare, as both sides have sought to gain control over key cities and population centers. This has involved close-quarters combat, with both sides making use of buildings, tunnels, and other structures for cover and concealment.

Artillery and rocket attacks: Both Ukrainian government forces and separatist forces have made use of artillery and rocket attacks in the conflict, targeting key infrastructure and civilian areas. These attacks have caused significant damage and loss of life, and have been a major source of civilian casualties and displacement.

Guerilla tactics: Separatist forces in the Donbas region have made use of guerilla tactics, including ambushes, hit-and-run attacks, and sabotage, to disrupt Ukrainian government operations and maintain control over territory. These tactics have proven effective in some cases, making it difficult for Ukrainian forces to gain a foothold in the region.

Cyber warfare: The conflict in Ukraine has also involved a significant amount of cyber warfare, with both sides making use of hacking and other tactics to gain intelligence and disrupt operations. This has included attacks on government and military networks, as well as on civilian infrastructure such as power grids and banking systems.

Special forces operations: Both Ukrainian government forces and separatist forces have employed special forces in the conflict, with these units carrying out reconnaissance, sabotage, and other operations behind enemy lines. These operations have been particularly effective in disrupting enemy supply lines and command and control structures.

Unmanned aerial vehicles (UAVs): Both sides in the conflict have made use of UAVs, or drones, for reconnaissance and other purposes. This has allowed for more precise targeting of enemy forces and infrastructure, and has also provided valuable intelligence for military commanders.

Hybrid warfare: The conflict in Ukraine has been characterized by what some analysts have called "hybrid warfare," involving a range of military, political, and economic tactics aimed at undermining the other side's position. This has included the use of propaganda, disinformation, and economic sanctions, as well as military operations on the ground.

Conclusion

The conflict in Ukraine has been marked by a range of military operations and tactics, reflecting the complex nature of the conflict and the competing interests at play. While some of these tactics have been effective in achieving military objectives, they have also caused significant damage and loss of life, and have had a devastating impact on civilian populations. As the conflict continues, it remains to be seen which tactics will ultimately prove decisive in determining the outcome.

# Role of international support

The conflict in Ukraine has not only been a domestic issue but has also attracted international attention and support. The involvement of various countries and international organizations has had a significant impact on the conflict, shaping its course and outcomes. This section will explore the role of international support in the conflict in Ukraine.

Russian support for separatists: Perhaps the most significant international support in the conflict has been the support provided by Russia to separatist forces in eastern Ukraine. This support has included the provision of weapons, military equipment, and training, as well as financial and logistical support. Russia has also been accused of providing direct military support, including sending troops and military advisors to the conflict zone. This support has played a major role in enabling separatist forces to gain control over territory and hold off Ukrainian government forces.

Western support for Ukraine: In response to Russian support for separatists, a number of Western countries have provided support to Ukraine. This has included the provision of military and non-military aid, such as weapons, equipment, training, and financial assistance. Western countries have also imposed economic sanctions on Russia in response to its actions in Ukraine. This support has been critical in enabling Ukraine to resist Russian aggression and defend its territorial integrity.

Role of NATO: The North Atlantic Treaty Organization (NATO) has also played a role in the conflict in Ukraine. While NATO has not intervened militarily, it has provided support to Ukraine in a number of ways, including the provision of non-lethal military aid and training. NATO has also increased its military presence in Eastern Europe in response to the conflict, and has conducted military exercises in the region as a show of support for its allies.

Role of the United Nations: The United Nations has been involved in efforts to resolve the conflict in Ukraine since it began. The UN has called for a ceasefire and has facilitated talks between the parties to the conflict. The UN has also provided humanitarian assistance to those affected by the conflict, including refugees and internally displaced persons (IDPs).

Role of the OSCE: The Organization for Security and Cooperation in Europe (OSCE) has also played a significant role in the conflict in Ukraine. The OSCE has been involved in efforts to monitor the ceasefire and has facilitated talks between the parties to the conflict. The OSCE has also played a role in monitoring and reporting on human rights abuses in the conflict zone.

Role of other countries: A number of other countries have also been involved in the conflict in Ukraine, providing support to either the Ukrainian government or separatist forces. These countries include Belarus, Kazakhstan, and Serbia, among others. The involvement of these countries has further complicated the conflict and made it more difficult to resolve.

Conclusion

The role of international support in the conflict in Ukraine has been significant, with various countries and organizations providing support to either the Ukrainian government or separatist forces. While this support has been critical in shaping the course and outcomes of the conflict, it has also been a source of controversy and tension between the parties involved. As the conflict continues, the role of international support will likely continue to be an important factor in determining its course and outcomes.

# Civil society resistance against occupation

The occupation of Donbas and the annexation of Crimea have resulted in significant challenges for the civilian population in the affected areas. However, the conflict has also spurred civil society resistance against the occupation, with individuals and groups actively opposing the actions of the separatist forces and the Russian government. This section will explore the various forms of civil society resistance against occupation that have emerged in Ukraine.

Civic initiatives: Civic initiatives have emerged across Ukraine in response to the conflict, with citizens taking an active role in opposing the occupation of Donbas and the annexation of Crimea. These initiatives include the formation of volunteer groups, community-based organizations, and online communities that provide support to affected individuals and communities. Some of these initiatives also engage in advocacy work and public awareness-raising campaigns aimed at raising awareness of the conflict and the human rights abuses taking place.

Grassroots activism: Grassroots activism has also emerged as a form of civil society resistance against the occupation. This includes protests, demonstrations, and other forms of direct action taken by individuals and groups to oppose the occupation and support the rights of affected populations. These actions have been met with repression and violence by separatist forces and Russian authorities, but have also been instrumental in raising public awareness and putting pressure on the government to take action.

Human rights monitoring: A number of human rights monitoring groups have emerged in Ukraine in response to the conflict, with the aim of documenting human rights abuses and violations committed by separatist forces and Russian authorities. These groups provide evidence-based reports to international human rights organizations and advocacy groups, as well as to the Ukrainian government, in order to hold those responsible accountable for their actions.

Media and information dissemination: Media and information dissemination have also played a critical role in civil society resistance against the occupation. Independent media outlets have emerged in Ukraine, providing alternative news coverage and critical analysis of the conflict, as well as exposing human rights abuses and other violations. Social media platforms have also been instrumental in disseminating information and organizing civil society responses to the conflict.

International solidarity: Civil society resistance against occupation has also been supported by international solidarity. International human rights organizations, advocacy groups, and other civil society actors have supported the efforts of Ukrainian civil society groups in opposing the occupation, providing funding, expertise, and advocacy support.

Conclusion

The occupation of Donbas and the annexation of Crimea have resulted in significant challenges for the civilian population in the affected areas. However, civil society resistance against the occupation has emerged as an important factor in the conflict, with individuals and groups actively opposing the actions of the separatist forces and the Russian government. These forms of resistance have taken many different forms, from civic initiatives to human rights monitoring to media and information dissemination. While the challenges faced by civil society groups in Ukraine are significant, their efforts have been instrumental in raising public awareness of the conflict, exposing human rights abuses, and putting pressure on the government to take action.

48

# Social and economic impacts of the conflict

The conflict in Ukraine, particularly the occupation of Donbas and the annexation of Crimea, has had significant social and economic impacts on the country. This section will explore some of the major effects of the conflict on Ukrainian society and its economy.

Displacement and migration: The conflict has resulted in significant displacement and migration, with hundreds of thousands of people forced to flee their homes due to the fighting. According to the United Nations Refugee Agency (UNHCR), as of 2021, there were more than 1.5 million internally displaced persons (IDPs) in Ukraine, with an additional 200,000 refugees who had fled to other countries. The displacement and migration have had significant social and economic impacts, disrupting family structures and communities, and straining the resources of the host communities.

Humanitarian crisis: The conflict has also resulted in a humanitarian crisis in the affected areas, with many people struggling to access basic necessities such as food, water, and healthcare. The fighting has damaged critical infrastructure such as hospitals and water treatment facilities, exacerbating the crisis. The Ukrainian government and international aid organizations have provided assistance, but the needs are significant, and many people continue to suffer.

Economic decline: The conflict has had a significant impact on Ukraine's economy, with the country experiencing a sharp decline in GDP since the onset of the conflict. The annexation of Crimea, which was a major economic center, has had a particularly significant impact, with the loss of industries such as tourism and agriculture. The fighting in Donbas has also disrupted economic activity

# Adaptation to the new reality

The conflict in Ukraine has forced the country to adapt to a new reality. The annexation of Crimea and the occupation of Donbas have fundamentally altered the geopolitical landscape in the region, and Ukraine has had to adjust to this new reality.

Diplomatic efforts: The Ukrainian government has engaged in a range of diplomatic efforts to address the conflict, both through bilateral and multilateral channels. The country has sought support from the international community, particularly from the European Union (EU) and the United States, and has worked to build alliances with other countries in the region, such as Poland and Lithuania. Ukraine has also been involved in negotiations with Russia and the separatist groups in Donbas, in an attempt to find a peaceful resolution to the conflict.

Military modernization: The conflict has highlighted the need for Ukraine to modernize its military and improve its capabilities. The Ukrainian armed forces have been engaged in a range of operations, from counter-insurgency operations in Donbas to providing support to international peacekeeping missions. The government has invested in modernizing the armed forces, with a particular focus on improving its cyber capabilities, as well as its capacity to counter hybrid warfare.

Reforms and anti-corruption efforts: The conflict has also spurred a range of reforms and anti-corruption efforts in Ukraine. The country has sought to improve its governance structures and strengthen the rule of law, with a particular focus on combating corruption. The government has implemented a range of reforms in areas such as healthcare, education, and the judiciary, as well as anti-corruption measures such as the establishment of a specialized anti-corruption court.

Economic diversification: The conflict has highlighted the need for Ukraine to diversify its economy and reduce its reliance on industries such as mining and heavy industry, which are concentrated in Donbas. The government has sought to encourage foreign investment in other sectors, such as IT and agriculture, and has implemented a range of measures to improve the business environment and reduce corruption.

Civil society engagement: The conflict has also spurred greater engagement from civil society in Ukraine, with people mobilizing to provide assistance to those affected by the conflict and to advocate for reforms and human rights. Civil society organizations have played a critical role in providing humanitarian assistance and supporting IDPs, as well as in monitoring the human rights situation in the conflict-affected areas.

Cultural identity: The conflict has also highlighted the importance of cultural identity in Ukraine, particularly in the face of efforts by Russia to promote a pro-Russian identity in the occupied territories. Ukrainian cultural figures, such as writers and musicians, have played an important role in promoting Ukrainian identity and resisting Russian influence.

In conclusion, the conflict in Ukraine has had significant social and economic impacts on the country, but it has also forced the country to adapt to a new reality. The Ukrainian government has engaged in diplomatic efforts, modernized its military, implemented reforms and anti-corruption measures, diversified its economy, and encouraged civil society engagement. The conflict has also highlighted the importance of cultural identity in Ukraine and the need to promote and protect it in the face of external pressures.

# Community building and solidarity

One of the key features of the conflict in Ukraine has been the emergence of community building and solidarity initiatives. These have taken a range of forms, from grassroots organizations to national campaigns, and have played an important role in supporting those affected by the conflict and in fostering a sense of solidarity and unity among Ukrainians.

Humanitarian assistance: One of the most visible forms of community building has been the provision of humanitarian assistance to those affected by the conflict. NGOs, religious groups, and other civil society organizations have played a critical role in providing food, shelter, and other essential supplies to displaced persons, as well as to those living in conflict-affected areas.

Volunteerism: Volunteerism has also emerged as an important form of community building. Ukrainians from all walks of life have volunteered their time and skills to support the military, provide assistance to displaced persons, and engage in other forms of community building. This has included everything from providing medical assistance to building homes for displaced families.

National campaigns: A range of national campaigns have also emerged in response to the conflict. These have included campaigns to raise funds for humanitarian assistance, as well as campaigns to promote Ukrainian identity and unity. One example is the "I am a Ukrainian" campaign, which started as a social media hashtag and quickly gained traction as a symbol of national unity and resilience.

Cultural events: Cultural events have also played an important role in building community and solidarity. Music festivals, art exhibitions, and other cultural events have provided opportunities for Ukrainians to come together and celebrate their shared culture and heritage. These events have often been organized in partnership with civil society organizations and have helped to raise awareness about the conflict and its impact on Ukrainian society.

Community engagement: Community engagement has also emerged as a critical component of community building and solidarity. This has included everything from neighborhood watch programs to community-led initiatives to support vulnerable groups such as the elderly, women, and children. These initiatives have been important in building resilience and fostering a sense of community ownership over the response to the conflict.

Social media: Social media has also played a key role in community building and solidarity. Ukrainians have used social media to share information about the conflict, to organize protests and other forms of civic engagement, and to connect with other Ukrainians both within the country and in the diaspora. Social media has helped to amplify voices of those affected by the conflict and has facilitated the sharing of information and resources.

In conclusion, community building and solidarity initiatives have played an important role in the response to the conflict in Ukraine. These initiatives have been critical in providing humanitarian assistance, promoting national unity and identity, fostering cultural engagement, and building resilience at the community level. As the conflict continues, it is likely that community building and solidarity initiatives will remain important in supporting those affected by the conflict and in promoting a sense of unity and resilience among Ukrainians.

## Trauma and coping mechanisms

The conflict in Ukraine has had a significant impact on the mental health and well-being of those affected by the violence and displacement. The trauma caused by the conflict has been profound, and individuals and communities have had to develop coping mechanisms to deal with the emotional and psychological effects of the violence.

Trauma: The trauma caused by the conflict has been both physical and psychological. For those who have experienced violence first-hand, the trauma can be acute and long-lasting. Witnessing violence, being forced to flee one's home, and living in a state of uncertainty and fear can all contribute to trauma. Trauma can manifest in a range of symptoms, including anxiety, depression, and post-traumatic stress disorder (PTSD).

Coping mechanisms: In response to the trauma caused by the conflict, individuals and communities have developed coping mechanisms to deal with the emotional and psychological effects of the violence. Some of the most common coping mechanisms include seeking social support, engaging in physical activity, and practicing relaxation techniques such as meditation and deep breathing. Religion and spirituality have also been important coping mechanisms for many Ukrainians.

Mental health services: Mental health services have been limited in Ukraine, particularly in the conflict-affected areas of the country. The lack of access to mental health services has made it difficult for those who have experienced trauma to receive the support they need. However, there are a number of organizations that are working to address this issue, including NGOs and international organizations that provide mental health services and support to those affected by the conflict.

Stigma: Despite efforts to raise awareness about the importance of mental health, stigma remains a significant barrier to seeking help. Many Ukrainians continue to view mental illness as a weakness or a personal failing, which can make it difficult for individuals to seek help when they need it. Addressing stigma is an important step in improving access to mental health services and promoting mental health and well-being.

Community support: Community support has been a critical coping mechanism for those affected by the conflict. Families, friends, and neighbors have provided emotional support to those who have experienced trauma, and community-based organizations have played an important role in providing social support and promoting resilience.

Self-care: Self-care has also emerged as an important coping mechanism for those affected by the conflict. Taking care of oneself, both physically and mentally, can help to reduce the impact of trauma and promote resilience. This can include engaging in physical activity, practicing mindfulness and relaxation techniques, and seeking out social support.

In conclusion, the trauma caused by the conflict in Ukraine has had a significant impact on the mental health and well-being of those affected by the violence and displacement. Coping mechanisms, including seeking social support, engaging in physical activity, and practicing relaxation techniques, have been important in helping individuals and communities deal with the emotional and psychological effects of the violence. However, the lack of access to mental health services and the stigma associated with mental illness remain significant barriers to improving mental health and well-being in Ukraine. Addressing these issues will be critical in promoting resilience and supporting those affected by the conflict.

## Prospects for resolution and peace

The conflict in Ukraine has been ongoing since 2014, and while there have been efforts to reach a resolution and bring about peace, the situation remains complex and fraught with challenges. Despite the many obstacles, there are still prospects for resolution and peace in Ukraine. In this section, we will explore the various initiatives that have been undertaken to resolve the conflict and the prospects for achieving lasting peace.

Negotiations: Diplomatic negotiations have been a critical component of efforts to resolve the conflict in Ukraine. Negotiations have taken place at various levels, including between the Ukrainian government and the self-proclaimed separatist republics in Donbas, as well as between Ukraine, Russia, and other international actors. While negotiations have not yet resulted in a lasting peace agreement, they remain an important tool for resolving the conflict.

Minsk agreements: The Minsk agreements, signed in 2015, represent the most significant effort to date to bring about a peaceful resolution to the conflict in Ukraine. The agreements provide a framework for a ceasefire, the withdrawal of heavy weapons, and the implementation of political reforms in the conflict-affected areas of Ukraine. While the Minsk agreements have not been fully implemented, they remain an important basis for future negotiations.

Normandy format: The Normandy format is a diplomatic initiative involving the leaders of Ukraine, Russia, France, and Germany. The format was established in 2014 as a means of resolving the conflict in Ukraine, and has played a key role in diplomatic efforts to bring about peace. While the Normandy format has not yet resulted in a lasting peace agreement, it remains an important platform for negotiations and diplomatic efforts to resolve the conflict.

Humanitarian initiatives: Humanitarian initiatives have been an important component of efforts to address the needs of those affected by the conflict in Ukraine. This has included the provision of humanitarian aid to those affected by the violence and displacement, as well as efforts to address the social and economic impact of the conflict.

Role of international actors: International actors, including the United Nations and the Organization for Security and Cooperation in Europe (OSCE), have played an important role in efforts to resolve the conflict in Ukraine. The UN has been involved in humanitarian efforts, as well as diplomatic initiatives to bring about peace. The OSCE has been involved in monitoring the ceasefire, as well as efforts to promote political reforms and address human rights concerns.

Challenges: Despite the many initiatives that have been undertaken to resolve the conflict in Ukraine, there are still many challenges that must be overcome. One of the biggest challenges is the lack of trust between the various parties to the conflict. The conflict has also been complicated by the involvement of external actors, particularly Russia, which has been accused of providing military and financial support to the separatist rebels in Donbas.

Prospects for peace: Despite the challenges, there are still prospects for resolution and peace in Ukraine. The ongoing negotiations and diplomatic initiatives, as well as the involvement of international actors, provide hope that a peaceful resolution to the conflict can be achieved. However, this will require sustained efforts and a willingness on the part of all parties to work towards a lasting peace.

In conclusion, the conflict in Ukraine has been ongoing since 2014, and while there have been many initiatives to resolve the conflict and bring about peace, the situation remains complex and challenging. Negotiations, the Minsk agreements, the Normandy format, humanitarian initiatives, and the involvement of international actors have all played important roles in efforts to resolve the conflict. Despite the challenges, there are still prospects for resolution and peace in Ukraine, but this will require sustained efforts and a willingness on the part of all parties to work towards a lasting peace.

**Implications for regional and global security**

The conflict in Ukraine has far-reaching implications for regional and global security. The annexation of Crimea and the ongoing war in Donbas have destabilized the region, and the involvement of external actors has heightened tensions between Russia and the West. In this section, we will explore the implications of the conflict for regional and global security.

The conflict in Ukraine has challenged the post-Cold War order in Europe. The annexation of Crimea was the first time since World War II that a European state had forcibly annexed territory from another state. The use of military force to change borders is a violation of international law and the United Nations Charter. The annexation of Crimea has been widely condemned by the international community, and the West has imposed sanctions on Russia in response.

The conflict in Donbas has also raised concerns about the security of Ukraine's borders and the stability of the region. The war has been characterized by a range of tactics, including artillery shelling, sniper fire, and the use of heavy weapons. The conflict has resulted in the displacement of over

1.5 million people, and the humanitarian situation in the region is dire.

The involvement of external actors in the conflict has further complicated the situation. Russia has provided military support to the separatists in Donbas, and there have been reports of Russian troops fighting in the region. The West has provided economic and military assistance to Ukraine, and NATO has increased its presence in the region. The conflict has heightened tensions between Russia and the West, and there are concerns that the conflict could escalate into a larger confrontation.

The conflict in Ukraine has also raised concerns about the future of the post-Cold War security architecture in Europe. The Organization for Security and Cooperation in Europe (OSCE), which was established to promote security and cooperation in Europe, has played a key role in monitoring the conflict in Ukraine. However, the conflict has highlighted the limitations of the OSCE in preventing and resolving conflicts in the region.

The conflict in Ukraine has also had implications for global security. The annexation of Crimea has raised concerns about the future of the non-proliferation regime. Ukraine had given up its nuclear weapons in exchange for security assurances from Russia and the West. The annexation of Crimea has raised questions about the credibility of these assurances and the future of the non-proliferation regime.

The conflict in Ukraine has also raised concerns about the future of the international order. The conflict has highlighted the limits of international law and the challenges of enforcing it. The annexation of Crimea was a violation of international law, but the international community has been unable to reverse it. The conflict has also raised questions about the role of the UN Security Council in maintaining international peace and security.

The conflict in Ukraine has challenged the post-Cold War order in Europe and raised concerns about the future of regional and global security. The involvement of external actors has heightened tensions between Russia and the West, and there are concerns that the conflict could escalate into a larger confrontation. The conflict has also highlighted the limitations of international institutions in preventing and resolving conflicts. The resolution of the conflict in Ukraine will require a concerted effort from the international community to uphold the principles of international law and promote peace and stability in the region.

# Lessons learned and recommendations

The conflict in Ukraine has been a tragic and costly experience for all involved. It has highlighted the fragility of peace and the importance of international norms and institutions. In this section, we will explore the lessons learned from the conflict and provide recommendations for preventing and resolving similar conflicts in the future.

One of the key lessons from the conflict in Ukraine is the importance of early warning and prevention. The conflict in Ukraine was not sudden; it was the result of a long-term political and economic crisis. The international community failed to recognize the warning signs and prevent the conflict from escalating. The conflict highlights the need for early warning systems that can identify and respond to potential conflicts before they escalate.

Another lesson from the conflict is the importance of regional cooperation. The conflict in Ukraine has had significant implications for the security of the region, and it requires a regional solution. The conflict has highlighted the need for regional actors to work together to promote peace and security. Regional organizations such as the OSCE and the European Union (EU) have a critical role to play in promoting regional cooperation and preventing conflicts.

The conflict in Ukraine has also highlighted the importance of conflict resolution mechanisms. The conflict has been characterized by a lack of political will and trust, which has made it difficult to resolve. The conflict highlights the need for conflict resolution mechanisms that can promote dialogue, build trust, and address the root causes of the conflict.

The conflict in Ukraine has also highlighted the importance of international law and institutions. The annexation of Crimea was a violation of international law, but the international community has been unable to reverse it. The conflict highlights the need for international institutions such as the UN and the International Criminal Court (ICC) to play a greater role in preventing and resolving conflicts.

The conflict in Ukraine has also highlighted the importance of addressing the root causes of conflict.

The conflict was the result of a long-term political and economic crisis, which created conditions for the conflict to escalate. The conflict highlights the need for a comprehensive approach to conflict prevention that addresses the root causes of conflict, including poverty, inequality, and corruption.

Finally, the conflict in Ukraine has highlighted the importance of civil society in promoting peace and stability. Civil society played a critical role in Ukraine, providing humanitarian assistance, monitoring human rights violations, and promoting dialogue between conflicting parties. The conflict highlights the need for civil society to be empowered and supported in promoting peace and stability.

Based on these lessons, we provide the following recommendations for preventing and resolving conflicts:

Early warning and prevention: The international community should invest in early warning systems that can identify and respond to potential conflicts before they escalate.

Regional cooperation: Regional organizations such as the OSCE and the EU should work together to promote peace and security in the region.

Conflict resolution mechanisms: The international community should invest in conflict resolution mechanisms that can promote dialogue, build trust, and address the root causes of conflict.

International law and institutions: The international community should uphold the principles of international law and support international institutions such as the UN and the ICC in preventing and resolving conflicts.

Addressing the root causes of conflict: The international community should address the root causes of conflict, including poverty, inequality, and corruption, as part of a comprehensive approach to conflict prevention.

Empowering civil society: The international community should support civil society in promoting peace and stability, including by providing humanitarian assistance, monitoring human rights violations, and promoting dialogue between conflicting parties.

In conclusion, the conflict in Ukraine has been a tragic and costly experience for all involved. It has highlighted the importance of early warning, regional cooperation, conflict resolution mechanisms, international law and institutions, addressing the root causes of conflict, and empowering civil society. By learning from the conflict in Ukraine and implementing these recommendations, we can prevent and resolve similar conflicts in the future and promote peace and

# Reflections on the war and its consequences

The war in Ukraine, which began in 2014, has had profound and far-reaching consequences for the country and the region. The conflict has caused tens of thousands of deaths, displaced millions of people, and created a humanitarian crisis. It has also led to the annexation of Crimea by Russia and the occupation of parts of eastern Ukraine. The war has had social, economic, and political impacts on the country, and has implications for regional and global security. In this section, we will reflect on the war and its consequences, and discuss what can be learned from this experience.

One of the most significant consequences of the war in Ukraine has been the trauma experienced by those who have lived through it. The conflict has been marked by violence, displacement, and loss, and has had a profound impact on the mental health of those affected. Many people have experienced symptoms of post-traumatic stress disorder (PTSD) and depression, and have struggled to cope with the aftermath of the war. In some cases, people have turned to drugs and alcohol to numb the pain, or have become withdrawn and isolated from their communities.

Despite these challenges, there have been remarkable stories of resilience and solidarity in the face of adversity. Communities have come together to support each other, and civil society organizations have played an important role in providing assistance and advocacy. Ukrainian volunteers have also played a critical role in defending their country and pushing back against the Russian-backed separatists. Their bravery and dedication have inspired many people around the world, and have helped to create a sense of national unity and pride.

The war in Ukraine has also had significant economic impacts on the country. The conflict has disrupted trade and investment, and has led to the loss of valuable assets and resources. The annexation of Crimea has had a particularly devastating impact on the Ukrainian economy, as the region was an important source of revenue and industry. The war has also made it difficult for Ukraine to attract foreign investment and support, as many investors are wary of the country's instability and conflict.

Despite these challenges, there have been some signs of economic recovery in recent years. The

Ukrainian government has implemented reforms to strengthen the economy and attract investment, and has worked to diversify its trade partners. The country has also received financial support from international organizations such as the International Monetary Fund (IMF) and the European Union (EU). While these efforts are encouraging, there is still a long way to go to address the economic impacts of the war.

The war in Ukraine has also had significant political implications for the country and the region. The conflict has led to a rise in nationalist sentiment, and has created a sense of urgency around issues such as security, sovereignty, and territorial integrity. The Ukrainian government has worked to strengthen its ties with the West, and has sought to join institutions such as NATO and the EU. However, these efforts have been met with resistance from Russia, which sees Ukraine as part of its sphere of influence.

The conflict has also had implications for regional and global security. The annexation of Crimea by Russia has violated international law and undermined the principles of territorial integrity and sovereignty. The war has also highlighted the vulnerability of countries in the region to external aggression, and has underscored the importance of collective security measures such as NATO. The conflict has also strained relations between Russia and the West, and has created a sense of distrust and animosity that will take years to overcome.

In reflecting on the war in Ukraine, there are several lessons that can be learned. First, the importance of international law and norms cannot be overstated. The annexation of Crimea by Russia was a clear violation of international law, and should be condemned by the international community. Second, the importance of community building and solidarity cannot be underestimated. Despite the trauma and challenges faced by Ukrainians, they have come together to support each

# Final thoughts and call to action

As this book comes to a close, it is important to reflect on the lessons learned from the war in Ukraine and consider how we can use this knowledge to create positive change in the world.

One of the most important takeaways from this conflict is the destructive power of nationalism and the importance of addressing historical grievances in a constructive manner. The Russian annexation of Crimea and the subsequent conflict in Donbas were fueled by the narratives of historical injustice and the protection of ethnic minorities. These narratives were exploited by political leaders to stoke nationalist sentiments and justify their actions. As a result, thousands of lives were lost and communities were torn apart.

Another key lesson is the need for international cooperation and diplomacy in resolving conflicts. The war in Ukraine has been a test case for the effectiveness of international law and the role of regional and global actors in managing crises. The inability of the international community to prevent the annexation of Crimea and the subsequent conflict in Donbas highlights the limitations of the current international system. However, it also presents an opportunity for policymakers to consider new approaches to conflict prevention and resolution.

At the same time, the war in Ukraine has also highlighted the power of grassroots movements and civil society in promoting peace and social change. The emergence of volunteer battalions, community-driven humanitarian initiatives, and resistance movements have demonstrated the importance of collective action and solidarity in times of crisis. These movements have provided a glimmer of hope in an otherwise bleak landscape and have inspired similar efforts in other conflict-affected regions.

Looking forward, it is important to recognize that the consequences of the war in Ukraine will continue to shape the region and the world for years to come. The conflict has exposed the fragility of the post-Cold War order and the need for a new approach to regional and global security. It has also highlighted the urgency of addressing the underlying drivers of conflict, including economic inequality, political corruption, and historical grievances.

In conclusion, the war in Ukraine has been a tragic and sobering experience, but it has also provided important insights into the nature of conflict and the potential for positive change. As we move forward, it is important to build on these insights and work towards a more peaceful and just world. This will require a collective effort from policymakers, civil society, and individuals around the world. We must remain vigilant in our commitment to human rights, justice, and the rule of law, and strive to create a world in which conflict is resolved through dialogue and cooperation, rather than violence and division.

Dear Reader,

I am writing to express my sincere gratitude for taking the time to read "Under Fire: The War in Ukraine". It is my hope that this book has provided you with a deeper understanding of the conflict and its impact on the people of Ukraine.

The war in Ukraine has been a tragedy for all those affected by it. From the annexation of Crimea to the conflict in Donbas, the war has had far-reaching consequences for the region and the world. Through this book, I have attempted to provide a comprehensive chronicle of the events and highlight the human stories that often get overlooked in discussions of geopolitics and international relations.

I believe that it is essential to learn from history and to be informed about the challenges facing our world today. The war in Ukraine has demonstrated the need for international cooperation, diplomacy, and a commitment to human rights and justice. It has also highlighted the resilience of communities and the power of collective action.

I hope that this book has inspired you to reflect on the lessons learned from the war in Ukraine and to consider how we can work towards a more peaceful and just world. I believe that it is only through understanding and empathy that we can overcome the divisions and conflicts that threaten our societies.

Once again, thank you for taking the time to read "Under Fire: The War in Ukraine". I am grateful for your interest in this important topic and I hope that this book has been a valuable contribution to your understanding of the conflict.

Sincerely, David

*Dear Reader,*

*I am thrilled to announce the release of my latest book, "Toward a New World Order". As someone who has shown an interest in exploring the complex issues of our world, I believe that this book will be of great interest to you.*

*In "Toward a New World Order", I tackle some of the most pressing issues of our time, from climate change and economic inequality to political polarization and the rise of authoritarianism. Drawing on my years of research and experience, I offer a fresh perspective on these challenges and propose concrete solutions for building a more equitable, sustainable, and just world.*

*This book is not only an exploration of the problems we face, but also a call to action. I firmly believe that we can overcome the challenges of our time, but it will require collective action, collaboration, and a commitment to building a better future for all.*

*If you enjoyed "Under Fire: The War in Ukraine", I believe that "Toward a New World Order" will provide you with further insights and perspectives on the* issues that shape our world. I invite you to join me on this journey towards a more just and equitable world.

Thank you for your continued support and interest in my work.

Sincerely, David

www.ingramcontent.com/pod-product-compliance
Lightning Source LLC
Chambersburg PA
CBHW070316120526
44590CB00017B/2698